New Alan Wake 2: Complete User Guide on Night Springs Expansion

Mastering Night Springs: Unlocking the Dark Place, Gameplay Mechanics, Character Guides, Survival Strategies, Collectibles, Achievements, and Storyline Walkthroughs

Borden Gorge

Copyright

Disclaimer

This guide is a work of fiction and is not officially endorsed or affiliated with Remedy Entertainment or any other copyright holders of Alan Wake 2. The guide is intended for entertainment purposes only and does not reflect the views or opinions of the game's developers or publishers. All trademarks and copyrights are property of their respective owners.

Table Of Contents

Chapter 1

Welcome to Night Springs (Introduction to the Expansion and Game Basics)

The psychological horror game Alan Wake 2 invites you to explore the deepest recesses of the human psyche. With its brand-new story, innovative gameplay elements, and spine-tingling atmosphere, the Night Springs expansion ushers in a new chapter in the Alan Wake series.

This chapter will walk you through the fundamentals of the game, take you on a tour of the Night Springs expansion, and provide crucial advice to get you going.

Narrative and Scenery

The fictitious hamlet of Night Springs, a sleepy, picturesque settlement cloaked in mystery, serves as the setting for the novel Night Springs. The narrative centers on best-selling novelist Alan Wake, who is experiencing writer's block and is trying to figure out what is going on in the town when odd things start happening. As Alan explores the mystery further, he learns that the boundaries between fiction and reality have been blurred by his most recent literary endeavor.

Fundamentals of Gameplay

Third-person shooter Alan Wake 2 places a lot of focus on combat, exploration, and narration. To help you get started, here are the fundamental gaming mechanics:

- Movement: Alan can sprint, leap, and run to get around.
- Combat: Defeat adversaries by using a range of weaponry, such as flare guns and pistols.
- Lighting: Light sources, such as flashlights or streetlights, can repel and weaken attackers.
- Stealth: To avoid conflicts, sneak past opponents without being seen.

Night Springs Growth

The Night Springs addition adds new narratives, characters, and gameplay elements to the original game. Here's what to anticipate:

- New Storyline: Discover a brand-new tale that delves into Night Springs's shadowy past.
- New Characters: Get to know new rivals and friends, each with their secrets and goals.
- New Weapons and Abilities: Use new tools to your advantage in battle and exploration.

Advice and Techniques

To help you get started in Night Springs, consider these crucial pointers:

- Investigate the surroundings to find hints and hidden mysteries.

- Make use of lights for stealth and fighting.

- Use your health and ammunition resources carefully.

- Pay attention to your surroundings since adversaries may strike out of nowhere.

Greetings from Night Springs, a trip into the deepest recesses of the human psyche. You're now prepared to take on the next difficulties thanks to this guidance. Stay tuned as we explore the plot and primary goals in the next chapter!

Chapter 2

Opening the Shadow World(Recognizing the Main Goals and Storyline)

We presented the Night Springs expansion and the universe of Alan Wake 2 to you in Chapter 1. It's time to go more into the plot and primary goals that form the foundation of the game's tale now.

Narrative

After the events of the original game, when the protagonist Alan Wake has been experiencing writer's block, the Night Springs expansion takes place. His missing wife Alice sends him an enigmatic letter that takes him to the sleepy village of Night Springs. The boundaries between fiction and reality are blurred when Alan explores the town's mysteries further and learns that his most recent literary endeavor, "The Dark Place," has come to pass.

Principal Goals

Finding Alice and learning the truth about the odd happenings in the town are your two major goals in Night Springs. To do this, you must:

1. *Discover Night Springs*: Look about the community for hints, trade secrets, and buried artifacts that disclose the town's sinister past.
2. *Uncover the Mystery of The Dark Place*: Enter the universe of Alan's most recent literary

endeavor and confront the evil that has engulfed the community.

3. *Rescue Alice*: Track down Alice and free her from the evil forces' grasp.

4. *Defeat the Enemies of Light*: Engage in combat with the Taken, the Wraith, and other otherworldly adversaries, as well as other forces of evil.

Important Characters

The following important figures will either help or impede your progress:

1. *Alan Wake*: The main character, is a best-selling writer with writer's block.

2. *Alice Wake*: Alan's wife who vanished and whose enigmatic letter initiates the Night Springs events.

3. *Sheriff Sarah Breaker*: An ally in Alan's quest to discover the truth is a local sheriff.

4. *Dr. Emma Taylor*: An enigmatic scientist with information on The Dark Place.

Advice and Techniques

The following are some crucial pointers to assist you in advancing the game:

1. *Observe your surroundings*: Secrets and clues may be found right in front of you.

2. *Make sensible use of your flashlight*: Light sources may disclose secret routes and weaken adversaries.

3. *Manage your resources*: To conquer obstacles, save your health and ammunition.

4. *Solve riddles*: To access additional sections, decipher cryptic messages, and solve puzzles.

We've opened the dark place in this chapter, exposing the plot and primary goals that form the core of the game's narrative. You're now prepared to take on the problems that lie ahead thanks to this information. Stay tuned as we explore the controls and gameplay aspects in the next chapter!

Chapter 3

Controls and Gameplay Mechanics (Gaining Combat, Puzzle-Solving, and Movement Skills)

We looked at the plot and primary goals of the Night Springs expansion in Chapter 2. It's now time to explore the controls and gameplay concepts that will guide you through Alan Wake 2's universe.

Mechanisms of Movement

In the third-person, Alan Wake 2 offers the following movement mechanics:

- Strolling - Jogging - Leaping - Squatting

Regulators:

- PC: Arrow keys or W, A, S, and D keys
- Left analog stick on the console

Battle Mechanisms

In Alan Wake 2, combat is an essential part of the gameplay. You must become proficient in the following mechanics:

- Swapping weapons - Taking aim and firing

- Melee assaults

- Block and dodge mechanisms

Regulators:

- Console: Face buttons and the right analog stick - PC: Mouse and keyboard

Puzzle-Solving Principles

A key component of the gameplay is solving puzzles, which calls on you to:

- Interpret coded communications
Address environmental riddles
- Use objects and instruments to get around barriers

Regulators:

- PC: Keyboard and mouse
- Console: Analog sticks and face buttons

Extra Hints and Techniques:

Utilize cover mechanisms to evade enemy fire; use stealth techniques to slip past adversaries unnoticed; carefully manage your resources, like as health and ammunition; and try out a variety of weapons and methods to see which ones work best for you.

We've reviewed the key controls and gameplay concepts in this chapter to help you go about Alan Wake 2's universe. You're now prepared to take on the problems that lie ahead thanks to this information. We'll get into the character guides in the next part, covering Alan Wake's talents as well as the friends and foes you'll face. Keep checking back!

Chapter 4

Character Guides (Alan Wake, His Allies, and the Mysterious Figures)

The gaming mechanics and controls that propel the action in Alan Wake 2 were examined in Chapter 3. It's time to explore the people that makeup Night Springs' cast of characters.

Alan Wake

- Character: successful novelist and protagonist - Dealing with writer's block and trying to find his wife Alice - Main weapon: flashlight - Capable of dodging and blocking blows

comrades

- Dr. Emma Taylor - Mysterious scientist - Knows about The Dark Place and its mysteries - Offers cryptic counsel and guidance - Sheriff Sarah Breaker - Local law enforcement official - Helps Alan learn the truth - Provides direction and assistance

Unidentified Figures

The Wraith is a supernatural being who wants to take credit for Alan's work and can take control of and inhabit other people.
- The Taken - People engulfed in gloom - Support the Wraith - Will do whatever it takes to get Alan's writing

Extra Personas

The events of Night Springs are initiated by the disappearance of Alice Wake, Alan's missing wife. Odin Anderson, a mysterious entity connected to The Dark Place, provides advice, although it is unclear what his genuine objectives are.

Advice and Techniques

- Develop connections with allies to get access to fresh skills and perspectives. Alan's flashlight may be used to repel and weaken adversaries. Watch out for enigmatic individuals since you never know what their genuine motivations are.

We've looked at the characters in Alan Wake 2 who drive the plot and gameplay in this chapter.

Now that you know this, you may explore Night Springs' world and learn its mysteries with more ease. Stay tuned as we explore survival tactics and advice for conquering obstacles in the next chapter!

Chapter 5

Survival Strategies (Tips and Tricks for Overcoming Challenges and Enemies)

We looked at the people who make up Night Springs' society in Chapter 4. It's time to start learning the survival techniques and methods that will enable you to defeat the obstacles and foes that lie ahead.

General Advice

- Use cover mechanisms to dodge enemy fire - Employ stealth techniques to slip past foes unnoticed - Conserve health and ammunition wherever feasible - Carefully manage your resources

Combat Techniques

Utilize your surroundings to your advantage; Use the dodge and block principles to evade enemy assaults; Swap between weapons to take advantage of flaws in the opposition; Use a flashlight to weaken and repel opponents

Adversarial tactics

The Taken: - Aim for the head to take down swiftly; - Repel with spotlights
The Wraith: - Stun with strong strikes; - Steer out of confrontation whenever you can

Strategies for Solving Puzzles

- Be aware of your surroundings - Use objects and gadgets to get past barriers - Interpret cryptic messages to access additional locations

Extra Advice

- Be aware of your surroundings to prevent surprises - Make the most of your friends - Try out various tactics to see which ones work best for you

We've gone over the survival tactics and advice in this chapter to assist you defeat Night Springs' obstacles and adversaries. Now that you know this, you're more prepared to take on the darkness. We'll get into the milestones and collectibles in the universe of Alan Wake 2 in the next chapter. Keep checking back!

Chapter 6

Achievements and Collectibles (Finding Hidden Items and Earning Rewards)

We looked at several survival techniques and advice in Chapter 5 to assist you get over Night Springs's difficulties. It's now time to explore the accomplishments and goodies in the Alan Wake 2 universe.

Gatherings

- Manuscript Pages: - Spotted throughout the game - Offer insights and a background

Coffee Thermos: - Situated in difficult-to-reach places - Unlock exclusive benefits

- Signs of Night Springs:

Concealed in obvious sight

- Share unknown facts about the place

Successes

- Finish the game on various difficulty settings - Locate every collectible
- Finish designated assignments and challenges
- Unlock exclusive benefits and incentives

How to Locate Collectibles

Investigate off the beaten route

- Use your flashlight to see objects that are concealed.
- Watch for any suspicious items or hints.

Advice on Achieving Your Goals

- Complete the game more than once to obtain new achievements.
- Try out several approaches to overcome obstacles.
- Monitor your progress and modify your gameplay as necessary.

Awards

Unlock unique content and get access to unique features.

- Improve the way you experience gaming

We've looked at the collectibles and milestones in the Alan Wake 2 universe in this chapter. Now that you know this, you may use your newfound knowledge to locate hidden objects and get prizes that will improve your gaming. We'll get into the more complex methods and approaches in the next chapter, which will improve your gaming. Keep checking back!

Chapter 7

Exploring Night Springs (Finding My Way Around the Town, Its Secrets, and Side Trips)

We looked at the artifacts and accomplishments in the world of Alan Wake 2 in Chapter 6. It's time to explore Night Springs itself now, learning about its mysteries and side missions.

Getting Around Town

Investigate the town's several areas

- Uncover undiscovered locations and regions

- Use your flashlight to find hints and secret routes.

Clues and Side Projects

Find out about the town's troubled past; assist the locals in their hardships; and learn the trade secrets of the nearby companies

Some Advice for Visiting Night Springs

- Take your time, looking around every corner. Speak with the locals to learn about their experiences.
- Apply cunning to answer riddles and open up new places.

Adjacent Tasks

Discover the mysteries of the ancient home on the hill; - Assist a struggling writer with his work; - Help the local sheriff with a fascinating case.

Awards

- Get access to unique content - Unlock new gear and weaponry - Improve the gaming experience

We have investigated the town of Night Springs in this chapter, learning about its mysteries and side missions. Now that you know this, you may explore the town like an expert and find all of its hidden treasures. We'll get into the more complex methods and approaches in the next chapter, which will improve your gaming. Keep checking back!

Chapter 8

Beyond the Lake House (Preparing for the Next Expansion and Future Content)

We investigated the town of Night Springs in Chapter 7, learning about its mysteries and side missions. It's time to go beyond the town now and get ready for the next expansion and new content.

Lake House

Holds the key to opening up new narratives and gameplay mechanics;-Is a mystery area with mysteries to discover;-It will be essential to the future expansion

Getting Ready for the Upcoming Growth

- Finish the main plot and all side missions - Gather all text pages and coffee thermoses
- Improve your tools and skills.

upcoming content

- New characters and allies; - Novel plots and gameplay elements
- New adversaries and difficulties

Some Advice for Get Ready for the Next Expansion

- Discover every hidden place in the game - Finish all side missions and treasures

Try out various gaming philosophies and techniques.

Alan Wake 2's Future

Enhanced visuals and gaming mechanics; - New content updates and expansions; - A persistent plot with fresh turns

We've explored the Lake House and beyond in this chapter, laying the groundwork for the next expansion and content. Now that you know this, you're ready to tackle the next part of the Alan Wake 2 story. Keep your wits about you and your flashlight close at reach at all times—the world of Night Springs is full of surprises and hidden gems. Await Alan Wake 2's next episode with anticipation!

Chapter 9

Advanced Techniques and Strategies (Expert Advice for Experienced Players)

We explored the Lake House and other areas in Chapter 8, getting ready for the next expansion and content. It's time to move on to more complex moves and tactics meant for seasoned players.

Gaining Combat Proficiency

- Complex adversary strategies - Weapon combinations and switching
- Block and dodge mechanisms

Enhancing Discovery

- Effective navigational strategies
- Locations of hidden items - Solutions to environmental puzzles

Making the Most of Your Resources

- Managing health and ammunition - Improving tools and weaponry - Making effective use of supplies and equipment

Professional Advice and Techniques

- Taking use of your surroundings to your advantage - Sly maneuvers that go unnoticed by opponents -

How to Use a Flashlight Expertly

- Sophisticated methods for using flashlights
- Poor point aiming - Combinations of flashlights

We've discussed advanced tactics and strategies for seasoned players in this chapter. You'll be able to master fighting, exploration, and resource management with the help of this professional guidance, which will help you advance your gaming. Since there are always surprises in the realm of Night Springs, never forget to exercise caution and flexibility in unexpected circumstances. Await the release of Alan Wake 2's last chapter!

Chapter 10

Wrap-Up and Parting Thoughts (Recap, Review, and Looking Ahead to the Future of Alan Wake 2)

This last part will serve as a summary of our trip through Alan Wake 2, a look back at the most important lessons learned, and an outlook on the game's future.

Review

- We investigated Night Springs' universe, learning about its mysteries and side missions.

We explored the Lake House and beyond as we got ready for the next content and expansion.

- We became skilled gamers after mastering sophisticated tactics and methods.

Examine

We became adept at resource management, combat, exploration, and exploration. We learned how to find our way about the town and all of its hidden treasures. We learned how to get ready for the next expansion and other content.

Gazing Forward

Enhanced visuals and gaming mechanics; - New content updates and expansions; - A persistent plot with fresh turns

Alan Wake 2's future

- New figures that are allies
- New adversaries and difficulties
- New features and gameplay mechanics

Last Words

The game Alan Wake 2 will keep developing and expanding. There are many surprises and hidden gems in the Night Springs universe. Alan Wake 2 has a promising and exciting future.

We've summarized our trip, gone over the most important lessons learned, and discussed what lies next for Alan Wake 2 in this last chapter. We really hope you have had fun with this tutorial and will have more fun with the game. Since there are always surprises in the realm of Night

Springs, never forget to exercise caution and flexibility in unexpected circumstances. Happy gaming, and best of luck!

www.ingramcontent.com/pod-product-compliance
Lightning Source LLC
Chambersburg PA
CBHW070138230526
45472CB00004B/1587